es flowers ivy cactus rainbows seashells rocks mountains tree roots
getable plants vines lava rocks rock cliffs tree bark grass river rock
ouds pebbles sunset lakes moon icicles bamb   ston
pine cones houseplants rock cliffs rivers streams minerals reflections
s seaweed shadows twigs vines flowers ivy cactus rainbows seashel
ds seedlings fruit trees vegetable plants vines lava rocks rock cliffs tre
pools snow weeds clouds pebbles sunset lakes moon icicles bamboo
veins in leaves mud pine cones houseplants rock cliffs rivers stream
branches fall leaves seaweed shadows twigs vines flowers ivy cactu
moss lichen seed pods seedlings fruit trees vegetable plants vines lav
the earth waves tide pools snow weeds clouds pebbles sunset lake
les fish patterns coral veins in leaves mud pine cones houseplants roc
animals tree trunks branches fall leaves seaweed shadows twigs vine
ls petrified wood moss lichen seed pods seedlings fruit trees vegetabl
en leaves cracks in the earth waves tide pools snow weeds clouc
ea sponges rain puddles fish patterns coral veins in leaves mud pin
er wind blown sand desert animals tree trunks branches fall leave
cks mountains tree roots waterfalls petrified wood moss lichen seed
ee bark grass river rocks leaves fallen leaves cracks in the earth wave
oo ferns cracked stone rivers sea sponges rain puddles fish pattern
ms minerals reflections in water wind blown sand desert animals tre
ctus rainbows seashells rocks mountains tree roots waterfalls petrified
s lava rocks rock cliffs tree bark grass river rocks leaves fallen leave
t lakes moon icicles bamboo ferns cracked stone rivers sea sponge
pools snow weeds clouds pebbles sunset lakes moon icicles bamboo
moss lichen seed pods seedlings fruit trees vegetable plants reflectio

animals tree trunks branches fall leaves seaweed shadows twigs
waterfalls petrified wood moss lichen seed pods seedlings fruit trees
leaves fallen leaves cracks in the earth waves tide pools snow weeds
rivers sea sponges rain puddles fish patterns coral veins in leaves mu
water wind blown sand desert animals tree trunks branches fall lea
rocks mountains tree roots waterfalls petrified wood moss lichen seed
bark grass river rocks leaves fallen leaves cracks in the earth waves tid
ferns cracked stone rivers sea sponges rain puddles fish patterns co
minerals reflections in water wind blown sand desert animals tree trur
rainbows seashells rocks mountains tree roots waterfalls petrified wood
rocks rock cliffs tree bark grass river rocks leaves fallen leaves cracks
moon icicles bamboo ferns cracked stone rivers sea sponges rain pu
cliffs rivers streams minerals reflections in water wind blown sand dese
flowers ivy cactus rainbows seashells rocks mountains tree roots wate
plants vines lava rocks rock cliffs tree bark grass river rocks leaves
pebbles sunset lakes moon icicles bamboo ferns cracked stone river
cones houseplants rock cliffs rivers streams minerals reflections in w
seaweed shadows twigs vines flowers ivy cactus rainbows seashells
pods seedlings fruit trees vegetable plants vines lava rocks rock cliffs
tide pools snow weeds clouds pebbles sunset lakes moon icicles ba
coral veins in leaves mud pine cones houseplants rock cliffs rivers st
trunks branches fall leaves seaweed shadows twigs vines flowers ivy
wood moss lichen seed pods seedlings fruit trees vegetable plants v
cracks in the earth waves tide pools snow weeds clouds pebbles su
rain grass river rocks leaves fallen leaves cracks in the earth waves tid
ferns cracked stone rivers mountains tree roots waterfalls petrified woo

discovering nature's alphabet

Discovering
Nature's
Alphabet

Krystina Castella
and Brian Boyl

Heyday Books
Berkeley, California

Thank you to Joanne Chan Taylor for her insight and commitment, to Rebecca LeGates for imaginative layouts and book design, Jana and Molly Boyl for discovering the perfect J, David Losgren from the Los Angeles Arboretum for his encyclopedic knowledge of plants, and Alan and Janet Kupchick for sharing our love of nature and photography. Special thanks to publisher Malcolm Margolin for the support he gives to California artists.

Heyday Books, founded in 1974, works to deepen people's understanding and appreciation of the cultural, artistic, historic, and natural resources of California and the American West. It operates under a 501(c)(3) nonprofit educational organization (Heyday Institute) and, in addition to publishing books, sponsors a wide range of programs, outreach, and events.

To help support Heyday or to learn more about us, visit our website at www.heydaybooks.com, or write to us at P.O. Box 9145, Berkeley, CA 94709.

Library of Congress Cataloging-in-Publication Data
Castella, Krystina.
    Discovering nature's alphabet / Krystina Castella and Brian Boyl.
        p. cm.
    Includes bibliographical references.
    ISBN 1-59714-021-X (hardcover : alk. paper)
    1. Natural history—Juvenile literature. 2. English language—Alphabet
—Juvenile literature.   I. Boyl, Brian. II. Title.
    QH48.C37 2005
    508--dc22
                                                2005017857

Title page photos: Seaweed and shells on beach, Palm Beach, Florida. All three images were found on the same beach, at the same time, within ten feet of each other.

Book design by Rebecca LeGates

Orders, inquiries, and correspondence should be addressed to:
    Heyday Books
    P. O. Box 9145, Berkeley, CA 94709
    (510) 549-3564, Fax (510) 549-1889
    www.heydaybooks.com

Printed in Singapore by Imago

10 9 8 7 6 5 4 3 2 1

To Brian's mother, Eve Boyl-Ofstad, who
taught him how to see things differently...

...and to Krystina's parents, Marion and
Michael Castella, who have always
encouraged her creativity

Introduction

"Discovering nature's alphabet" is a playful adventure, a game of looking and seeing. Anyone can play.

Find letters by looking around the neighborhood, in a local park, at the beach, in a garden, at the zoo, on a hike, or while camping. At first, a forest or park might seem like a jumble of branches, leaves, flowers, and rocks, but letters will begin to emerge in nature's repetition, patterns, shapes, and brilliant colors.

If you like, take a camera on your quest. Photographs capture your discoveries and allow you to bring them home to share with friends. When you take your pictures, pay attention to scale, line, shape, texture, color, and framing, so that the letters will be clear and the pictures will be exciting. Over time you will acquire your own personal collection of all twenty-six letters.

We hope this exploration game broadens your smile, curiosity, sensitivity, and perception of the world around you.

Good luck in your adventures,

Krystina and Brian
www.discoveringnaturesalphabet.com

Branch in wildflower field, Lone Pine, California

Nature holds a secret world filled with hidden letters.

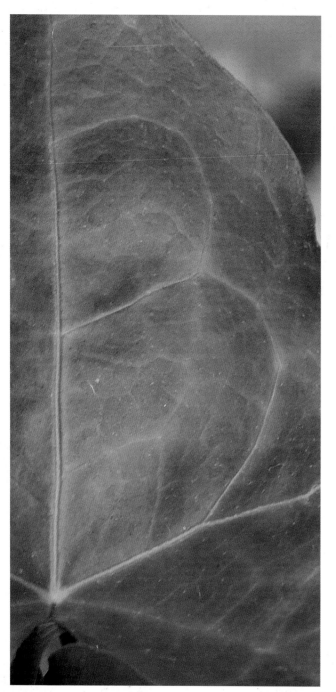
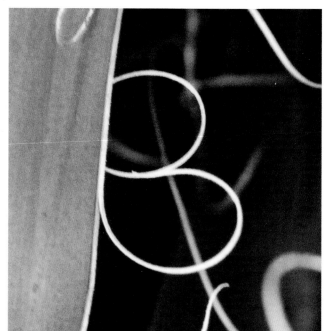

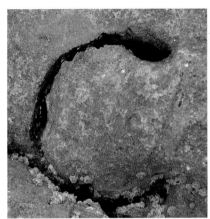

The best way to find them is to slow down and explore.

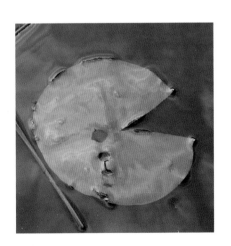

Look for the
building blocks
of letters in lines
and branches...

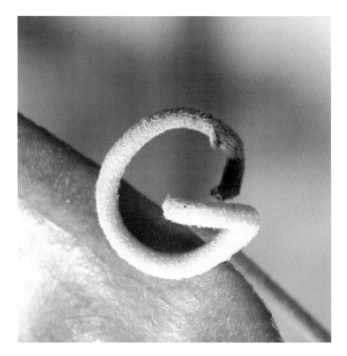

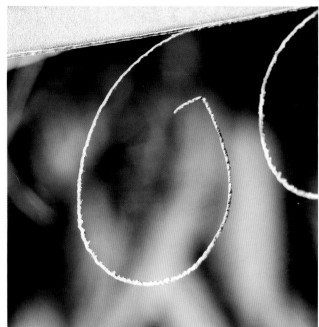

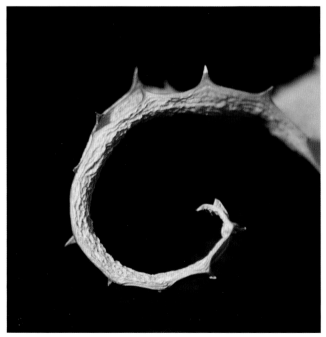

...or in curves and curls.

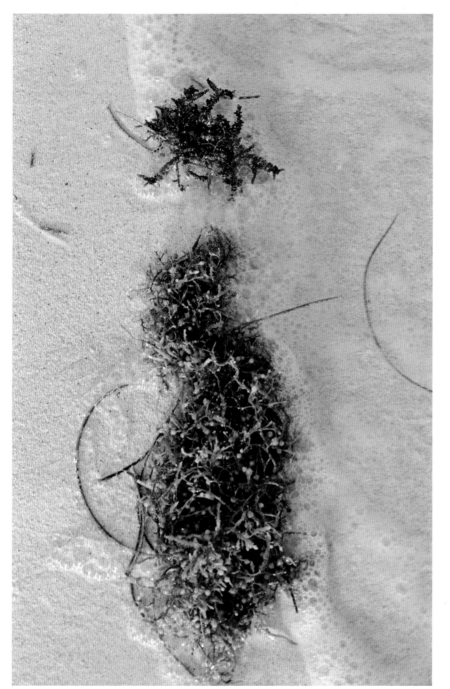
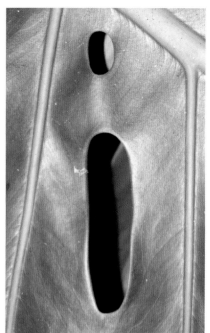

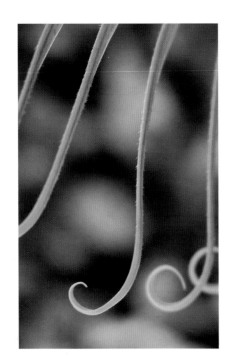

A letter might
hide until you
stand in just
the right place.

Nature makes letters in minutes, days...

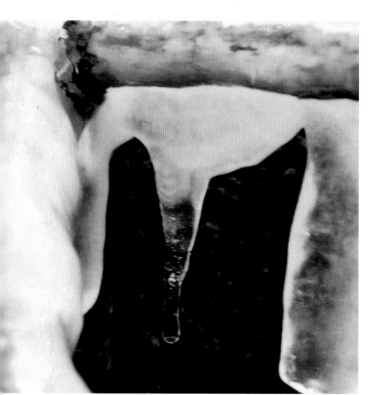

years…

or centuries.

They grow in flowers,

hang on trees,

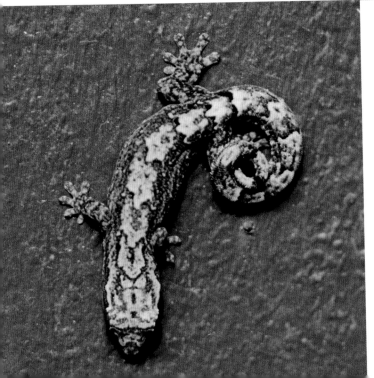

and are shaped

by animals.

One might sprout from a vine in spring,

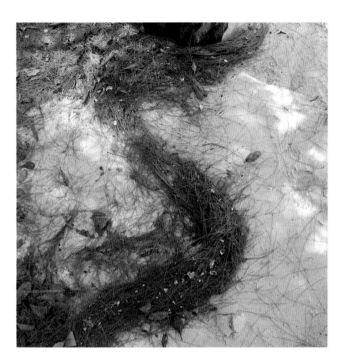 

or wash ashore on a summer beach.

One might appear in

autumn leaves,

or be etched in winter snow.

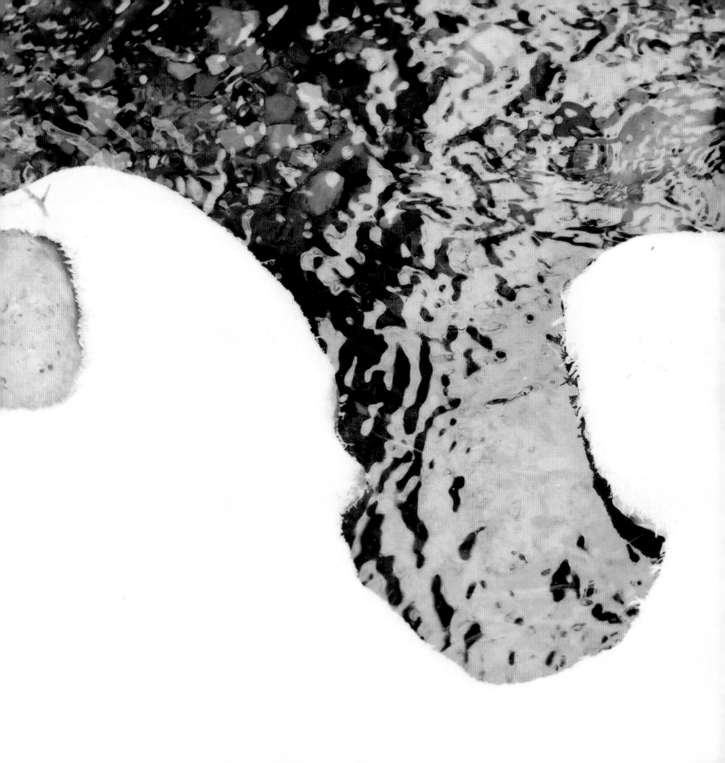

Letters can

be big

or small.

They are everywhere,

from the desert

to the ocean.

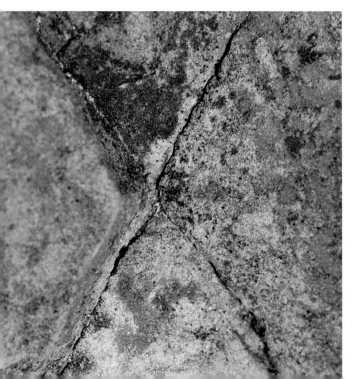

Nature's alphabet

is all around us,

just waiting to

be discovered.

Afterword

Discovering Nature's Alphabet was born as a hiking game that inspired us to slow down and absorb the intricate details in nature. Several years ago we were at Joshua Tree National Park, in Southern California. We looked up, and to our amazement we saw a tree that looked like the letter "Y." Then we noticed another "Y" off in the distance. We took a picture of our discovery, and then we asked each other, "Do you think we can find the whole alphabet in nature?" We decided to find out.

As time passed, we noticed that our "alphabet hunts" piqued the curiosity of children, who became excited about scouring a pine forest for the perfect "J" or crawling around a tide pool for that consistently elusive "Q." They began to really see nature.

In *Discovering Nature's Alphabet,* we hope to share this pastime, which has evolved into a way to encourage children to appreciate nature's beauty. The letters of the alphabet that we present in the photographs here were formed entirely by nature, untouched by human hands. The shots were found—not staged—and the photos are not retouched: Nature made them, we shot them, and that's it.

Branch Shadows, Montecito, California

Pine branches,
Los Angeles,
California

Vine on beach,
Bahia Honda,
Florida

Twig,
Key West,
Florida

Vein in ivy leaf,
San Marino,
California

Leaf fiber,
San Marino,
California

Fungus on tree
stump,
Key West,
Florida

Pink dahlia,
Victoria, B.C.,
Canada

Seedpod on
the beach,
Maui, Hawaii

Fallen palm
branch,
Maui, Hawaii

Seedpod
in snow,
Mount Whitney,
California

Tide pool rock,
Laguna Beach,
California

Lily pad,
Arcadia,
California

Moss on tree
trunk,
Mount Hood,
Oregon

Coral on lava
rock beach,
Maui, Hawaii

Grass, Bahia
Honda, Florida

Fungus on
tree trunk,
Key West,
Florida

Fallen seed-
pods,
Key West,
Florida

Day lily,
Arcadia,
California

Tree with moss,
Olympic
National Park,
Washington

Creeping
fig vine on
tree trunk,
Key West,
Florida

Tree root,
Maui, Hawaii

Cactus,
Anza Borrego
State Park,
California

Needleless
spruce in
winter,
Park City, Utah

Cactus thorns,
San Marino,
California

Mangrove
seedling,
Bahia Honda,
Florida

Vine,
Arcadia,
California

Yucca fiber,
San Marino,
California

Cactus tip,
San Marino,
California

Twigs on
beach,
Boca Raton,
Florida

Tree roots,
Maui, Hawaii

Birch in snow,
Cottonwood
Canyon, Utah

Palm tree,
Arcadia,
California

Seaweed washing ashore, Bahia Honda, Florida

Split-leaf philodendron, San Marino, California

Tide pool, Laguna Beach, California

Fern leaf, Escondido, California

Bean sprout, Arcadia, California

Fir tree, Mount Hood, Oregon

Onion sprout, Arcadia, California

Changing leaves, Los Angeles, California

Sycamore trees in park, Los Angeles, California

Eucalyptus branch, Arcadia, California

Coral on lava rock beach, Maui, Hawaii

Hemlock bark, Redwood National Park, California

Raindrops on leaf, Redwood National Park, California

Sea sponge on beach, Bahia Honda, Florida

Icicles on branch, Cottonwood Canyon, Utah

Pomegranate fruit, San Marino, California

Sweet gum branch, Los Angeles, California

Bamboo, San Marino, California

Palm trees, Arcadia, California

Rust on rock, Laguna Beach, California

Rocks in rock, Olympic National Park, Washington

Petrified wood, Petrified Forest National Park, Arizona

Flower, Arcadia, California

Lichen on tree, Jedediah Smith Redwoods State Park, California

Gecko on wall, Maui, Hawaii

Yucca vein, San Marino, California

Cactus with bud, San Marino, California

Leaf edge, Escondido, California

Succulent tip, San Marino, California

Grapevine, Arcadia, California

Tropical pine needles on beach, Boca Raton, Florida

Seedpod hanging in tree, Key West, Florida

 Cactus,
San Marino,
California

 Broken rock,
Santa Barbara,
California

 Sweet gum
tree in fall,
Los Angeles,
California

 Fallen bamboo leaves,
San Marino,
California

 Cactus wrapping around
tree trunk,
Key West,
Florida

 Quartz inlaid
rock,
Angeles
National
Forest,
California

 Burnt tree
trunk,
Kings Canyon
National Park,
California

 Limestone
deposits,
Yellowstone
National Park,
Wyoming

 Melting snow,
Cottonwood
Canyon, Utah

 Red rock
mountain,
Sedona,
Arizona

 Bird of paradise flower,
Montrose,
California

 Bamboo,
San Marino,
California

 Thorns,
Escondido,
California

 Ginkgo leaf,
Montrose,
California

 Shadow on
rock,
Montecito,
California

 Succulent in
lava rock,
San Marino,
California

 Saguaro at
dusk,
Saguaro
National Park,
Tucson, Arizona

 Starfish,
Long Beach,
California

 Driftwood
in lake,
Ochoco
National
Forest, Oregon

 Vine wrapping
around tree
trunk,
Boca Raton,
Florida

 Spider in web,
Maui, Hawaii

 Lichen-covered
rock,
Santa Barbara,
California

 Juniper,
Grand
Canyon
National Park,
Arizona

 Cactus tip,
San Marino,
California

 Tropical tree,
San Marino,
California

 Joshua trees,
Joshua Tree
National Park,
California

 Rock on
beach,
Laguna
Beach,
California

 Tree roots,
Angeles
National
Forest,
California

flowers ivy cactus rainbows seashells rocks mountains tree root
vegetable plants vines lava rocks rock cliffs tree bark grass river rock
clouds pebbles sunset lakes moon icicles bamboo ferns cracked ston
pine cones houseplants rock cliffs rivers streams minerals reflections i
seaweed shadows twigs vines flowers ivy cactus rainbows seashel
ds seedlings fruit trees vegetable plants vines lava rocks rock cliffs tre
pools snow weeds clouds pebbles sunset lakes moon icicles bambo
veins in leaves mud pine cones houseplants rock cliffs rivers stream
branches fall leaves seaweed shadows twigs vines flowers ivy cactu
moss lichen seed pods seedlings fruit trees vegetable plants vines lav
the earth waves tide pools snow weeds clouds pebbles sunset lake
es fish patterns coral veins in leaves mud pine cones houseplants roc
animals tree trunks branches fall leaves seaweed shadows twigs vine
s petrified wood moss lichen seed pods seedlings fruit trees vegetabl
en leaves cracks in the earth waves tide pools snow weeds cloud
ea sponges rain puddles fish patterns coral veins in leaves mud pin
er wind blown sand desert animals tree trunks branches fall leave
cks mountains tree roots waterfalls petrified wood moss lichen see
e bark grass river rocks leaves fallen leaves cracks in the earth wave
oo ferns cracked stone rivers sea sponges rain puddles fish patterr
ms minerals reflections in water wind blown sand desert animals tre
ctus rainbows seashells rocks mountains tree roots waterfalls petrifie
lava rocks rock cliffs tree bark grass river rocks leaves fallen leave
t lakes moon icicles bamboo ferns cracked stone rivers sea sponge
pools snow weeds clouds pebbles sunset lakes moon icicles bambo
moss lichen seed pods seedlings fruit trees vegetable plants reflectio

animals tree trunks branches fall leaves seaweed shadows twigs
waterfalls petrified wood moss lichen seed pods seedlings fruit trees
leaves fallen leaves cracks in the earth waves tide pools snow weed
vers sea sponges rain puddles fish patterns coral veins in leaves mu
vater wind blown sand desert animals tree trunks branches fall lea
ocks mountains tree roots waterfalls petrified wood moss lichen seed
bark grass river rocks leaves fallen leaves cracks in the earth waves ti
erns cracked stone rivers sea sponges rain puddles fish patterns co
minerals reflections in water wind blown sand desert animals tree trun
ainbows seashells rocks mountains tree roots waterfalls petrified woo
ocks rock cliffs tree bark grass river rocks leaves fallen leaves cracks
moon icicles bamboo ferns cracked stone rivers sea sponges rain pu
cliffs rivers streams minerals reflections in water wind blown sand dese
lowers ivy cactus rainbows seashells rocks mountains tree roots wate
plants vines lava rocks rock cliffs tree bark grass river rocks leaves
pebbles sunset lakes moon icicles bamboo ferns cracked stone river
cones houseplants rock cliffs rivers streams minerals reflections in v
eaweed shadows twigs vines flowers ivy cactus rainbows seashells
pods seedlings fruit trees vegetable plants vines lava rocks rock cliffs
ide pools snow weeds clouds pebbles sunset lakes moon icicles ba
coral veins in leaves mud pine cones houseplants rock cliffs rivers st
runks branches fall leaves seaweed shadows twigs vines flowers ivy
wood moss lichen seed pods seedlings fruit trees vegetable plants v
cracks in the earth waves tide pools snow weeds clouds pebbles su
ain grass river rocks leaves fallen leaves cracks in the earth waves ti
erns cracked stone rivers mountains tree roots waterfalls petrified woo